The 'Secret' Guide to Car Buying and Credit

101 things you should know to survive in the car buying and credit jungle

Joe Bananas

ISBN: 1515272648
ISBN–13: 978-1515272649

CONTENTS

INTRODUCTION

Randomly survey 100 people. Ask them to name one of the most negative shopping experiences they ever had in life. I'm willing to bet at least 85% will respond with "buying a car". This is a sad testament to a seriously flawed business model that still struggles to improve its tawdry image with the general public.

The automobile industry has worked overtime to earn the reputation of being viewed as a corrupt industry rife with dealer double talk, bait and switch, borderline fraudulent advertising created to get you on their lot and a multitude of other sins... all the bad parts of the Bible so to speak... deliberately intended to confuse and cheat the buyer whose only crime in all of this is wanting the hassle free experience of buying or leasing a new(er) car.

When driving into most dealerships what greets you, the buyer? As many as 15 salespeople staring at you – the next 'Up' (car dealer slang for the new customer that just arrived) – like hungry wolves.

This 'Welcome' is an old school car sales technique where managers way past their prime still believe that having a small army of salespeople hanging around outside the entrance is the best way to sell a car in the 21st century. Here's a radical idea for them to think over: Why not have 1 or 2 salespeople outside and the others at their desks making phone calls and doing something productive?

Why is the car buying process so difficult? It doesn't have to be but there are far too many managers and salespeople who have no respect whatsoever for what the buyer wants or needs. As a salesperson, I remember once being scolded by my sales manager who said, "You spend way too much time caring about what the buyer wants. Just sell them a car and get them out of here." What he failed to acknowledge was that 'listening' to the buyer resulted in me selling 23 cars that month!

Too often what the buyer asks for goes in one ear and out the other. For the dealer, it's all about giving minimal customer service and slamming them into whatever is in stock while hopefully collecting a fat commission during the process.

Until this old style way of selling is cleaned up forever, car salespeople will continue to be looked upon as vile toad–like creatures whose self-interest supersedes that of the customer.

The industry needs a complete overhaul with regard to how salespeople are compensated and how the customer should be treated. This isn't rocket science but old habits, particularly with this business model, die hard.

My goal in writing this book is to arm you with practical and relevant information so that you don't over pay for a vehicle, or give in to the pressure from clowns who think it's funny to force someone into buying a car they don't like. I've also included a few credit 'secrets' that are useful if you have other credit problems that need attention first.

I truly believe there is enough valuable information in this guide to help everyone who takes time to read its content. This book was not meant to be Shakespeare, just a car buying and credit survival map to get you home in one piece without being eaten by the sharks.

I wrote this for the average person who simply wants to be a better consumer without being taken advantage of. This book is an equalizer. I want you to keep more of your money in your pocket instead of giving it to the dealer.

In my ideal world, every buyer carries this guide with them when they go car shopping to show the dealer that Joe Bananas is there in spirit watching over his readers.

If you save money from using any of the 'secrets' I've revealed, please donate a portion of those savings to your local humane society to support their mission.

Good luck with your shopping and remember,

"In Bananas We Trust!"

Sincerely,

Joe Bananas

Why it takes so long to buy a car.

Most people are tricked into spending 4 or 5 hours, sometimes even longer, at the dealership to complete the purchase of their new car.

Why does this happen? Because dealers design the process to be that way on purpose. They want to wear you down. By doing this, it gives them an opportunity to get more of your money since you're not fully attentive to all the games they play which you'll learn in this book.

Most buyers hope to be at the dealership only a couple of hours. As the dealer finds ways to drag out the buying process, buyers get hungry, tired and anxious. After spending most of their day at the dealership, the exhausted buyer wants to end to the lengthy and complicated negotiation process as fast as possible.

Think of it, the more time you spend at the dealership negotiating with the dealer, the greater the probability that one of more of these things will happen as they break down your defenses:

1. You end up buying a car you really didn't want.

2. You overpay for the car that you bought.

3. You accept less for your trade-in.

4. You purchase expensive warranty and maintenance packages that add more profit to the dealer's bottom

line.

Before going car shopping, A) make sure to get a good night's sleep; B) have a good meal so that being hungry doesn't distract you from negotiating a good price; C) do research in advance to have some idea about your potential new car's color and options; and D) bring a friend or family member for moral support.

Did you get 2 sets of keys and a FULL tank?

If you are buying a used car, ask if it comes with 2 sets of keys (do the fobs to lock and unlock the doors work?) and a full tank of gas.

The salesperson is told to avoid this topic and let you assume these are included in the sale. Every extra dollar spent on providing these items reduces the dealer's profit and means a smaller commission to them.

With used cars there is usually only 1 key and just enough gas in the tank to drive off the lot.

Dealers surprise you with this fact *after* you've signed the purchase contact THEN make it sound like you should have known this all along.

After you sign the purchase contract they won't give you an extra key or full tank without a fight. Know how to play by the dealer's rules and you will always be a winner.

Dealer 'secret' warranties.

Dealers call them extended warranties, policy adjustments and other vague names meant to confuse you. The correct term is 'Technical Service Bulletin'.

Whenever a car has a defect that occurs after its written warranty expires, the manufacturer will rarely notify the consumer. Payoffs to Congress from lobbyists keep the government from forcing car manufacturers to disclose many major defects until they turn into a public relations disaster.

A secret warranty could be in effect for the new OR used car you plan to buy. Always perform research in advance to see if there are any Technical Service Bulletins that require a defect to be corrected at no cost you.

CarFax or AutoCheck. Which one is better?

A 'clean' CarFax is not a guarantee that the vehicle has not been in an accident. Also, an accident shown on CarFax could be minor and not negatively impact the quality of the car. CarFax and AutoCheck are helpful when negotiating car price.

Vehicle history reports rarely show the maintenance history. Having an inspection done on a used vehicle by YOUR mechanic prior to making a commitment to buy is important.

AutoCheck reports are usually better for the buyer than CarFax because it provides information about the vehicle in a clear and concise format that is easy to read. Most dealers believe that AutoCheck is better at reporting accidents.

Whenever possible try to get both a CarFax and AutoCheck to compare the information contained in each report.

A 'cookie' from the car dealer?

No, it's not an oatmeal raisin one. It's the kind that a car dealer attaches to their email so they know exactly when you opened it.

This is a tracking service offered to car dealers who buy their CRM (Customer Relationship Management) software from a company called VIN Solutions and probably exists in other similar programs sold by other companies as well.

If you ever opened an email and wondered why you were suddenly called by the salesperson a few minutes afterward that's why. The tracking cookie told them you read their email.

Opt out of such mailings and end this invasion of your privacy.

Dealer not responsive? Do this and they will.

Have a problem and the dealer is not responding? The squeaky wheel always gets the grease.

Make at least 3 attempts to get your complaint taken care of by the dealer. If you still aren't happy contact their corporate office and speak with a representative.

Nothing makes a dealer pay attention to you faster than getting a call from the people who control their franchise AND end-of-the year holdback money.

Decoding the 'VIN'.

VIN stands for 'Vehicle Identification Number' which is the sequence of 17 numbers and letters that an automobile manufacturer assigns to every vehicle.

The VIN tells you several things about a car: region of the world where the vehicle was manufactured (e.g. North America, Africa, Asia, etc.), country of origin (USA, Canada, Japan, etc.), airbag type, engine size, model year and trim level. The VIN is stamped into a plate that's mounted on the dashboard near the windshield or on the driver's side door jamb. It's also stamped on the engine's firewall.

Because I like to buy products where most of the manufacturing and assembly is done in the USA, I check the VIN to confirm this myself. To avoid being misled, visit this site to decode any VIN yourself: **http://www.vindecoder.net/**

MSRP or Invoice?
Don't pay
either one.

In the past uninformed buyers paid Manufacturer's Suggested Retail Price (MSRP), also known as 'full sticker'. Now with dealer pricing disclosed on the internet, buyers realize that paying full MSRP is a bad thing.

Tell the dealer you want to pay invoice. While this is lower than MSRP, a savvy buyer can end up paying way below invoice if they are a skilled negotiator and are willing to shop around for a dealer who will cooperate.

Dealers will whine that they incur a loss by selling to you at or below invoice and that isn't true. Think about it, does anyone stay in business selling their product at a loss?

Simply tell the dealer to recover their 'loss' from the next buyer who hasn't bought a copy of Joe Bananas 'Secret' Guide.

Leasing:
How to compute
your interest rate.

The 'money factor' is car dealer mumbo jumbo for 'interest rate'. They both mean the same.

Most people don't know how to convert their leasing money factor to an actual interest rate and tell if they are being charged fairly. Because of this, those with excellent credit and bad credit are equally over charged on the interest.

When leasing a car, ask what the 'money factor' is then multiply it by 2400. For example, if your money factor is .00121 your interest rate is 2.9% (.00121 x 2400 = 2.9%).

Before signing your lease contract check to make sure the money factor has not been increased without your knowledge. This 'mistake' happens often so pay attention.

Dealer holdback, their 'secret' 3% Profit.

Auto manufacturers withhold 3% of the MSRP and usually return it to dealers at the end of the year. It's called 'holdback'.

When a dealer cries to you they are not making a profit on your sale they assume you don't know about the holdback.

Smile and show them this page.

Lease payments based on MSRP? Nooo!!!

When leasing do NOT let the dealer distract you and calculate your monthly lease payment based on the full MSRP of the car.

If you let them do that, your monthly payment will generally be anywhere from $25 – $75 per month higher depending on the car and options that you choose.

Ask to see the invoice for the car you want to lease then negotiate the monthly payment based on invoice price or below invoice price and you'll save as much as $2,500 over the lease term.

Costco new car pricing ain't always better.

Costco offers 'pre–negotiated' new car prices through most dealers for their members. Depending on the vehicle, pricing is slightly above or below the Costco 'base price' which is what dealers refer to as their 'invoice price'.

While the Costco pricing is a nice benefit to have, this isn't always the best or the smartest way to buy a car.

Shoppers who dislike the hassle of negotiating settle for Costco member pricing. Another shopper willing to invest more time and energy will get a lower price most of the time. Their resulting savings could be as much as $1,500 more than the Costco 'no-hassle' price.

The decision is yours. Do you accept the Costco pricing, or do you negotiate to save more money?

Are you a 'brick' or a 'roach'?

In the car business a person with great credit (740 FICO or higher) is called a 'brick' while a person with bad credit (550 FICO and below) is called a 'roach'.

Bricks can buy or lease whatever they want with nothing down at very low interest rates. Bricks seldom have to prove their income while roaches need a sizeable down payment and proof of income to get a car loan approved.

Roaches pay insanely high interest rates of between 10% and 29%.

Car dealers love roaches because they have limited options and will pay higher prices which generate more profit for them.

Avoid warranties sold by the finance manager.

#14

The role of the finance manager at the dealership is to prepare your legal documents and try to upsell you by offering a selection of extended warranty and maintenance packages.

Say "No thanks" to these expensive packages because they are designed to generate huge commissions for the finance manager. Some of them make more than $20,000 per month(!) by convincing naïve buyers that this coverage is required.

Buy any additional coverage you need from somewhere else at a more competitive price.

Never make a down payment on a car lease!

When leasing you are required to pay the first month's payment along with tax, title and registration in order to drive the car off the lot.

Never make a large down payment on top of that; it will only lower your monthly payment by an extra $20 or so for every $1,000 that you put down.

Do what the wealthy do when leasing a car: take the down payment, divide it by 36 (because the standard lease term is 36 months) then add that amount to your monthly payment every month.

It serves the same purpose, plus you are keeping the other money in the bank to earn nominal interest instead of withdrawing it in a lump sum to give the dealer.

The wealthy leverage their money in various ways like this all the time; so should you.

Corvette deposit scam. No 'allocations'.

Buying a Corvette? General Motors issues 'allocations' (1 allocation = 1 Corvette) to dealers who meet certain sales standards for this specialty car. If the dealer sells enough Corvettes, the next model year General Motors will issue a letter increasing the number of allocations.

To get their hands on your money, dealers who <u>don't</u> have allocations will claim they do so that you will put down a large deposit. The dealership will hold this deposit for weeks, sometimes months, and lie to you that your car is in production.

After waiting several months and not getting their Corvette, the buyer eventually realizes the dealer never had any allocations to begin with and demands a refund. The lesson here: When ordering a high end Corvette, ask to see the dealer's letter from General Motors that they actually have allocations to draw against.

Negative equity
is like Viagra to
car dealers.

When you trade-in a car that you still owe money on, and the trade-in value is not enough to pay off the car, that excess amount is called 'negative equity'.

This amount has to be paid somehow and car dealers will happily tack it on to your new car loan which results in a higher loan amount and monthly payment.

A bigger loan means more profit to the dealership because they get a financing kickback from the lender. This is another reason why you must do everything you can to get the highest value possible for your trade.

Can you afford that monthly payment?

Dealers don't give a damn about you and whether you can afford to make the monthly payments. They only want to make a sale and will use every tactic possible *at your expense*.

Think about it: If you are struggling now to make timely payments of $300 a month on the car you already have, why let some silver tongued stranger sucker you into payments of $400 per month? That's a whopping 33% increase in your monthly car payment, or a 50% increase if they con you into a $450 per month payment.

You know your budget better than anyone else. Don't let a fast talking salesperson play on your emotions and rope you into a 5, 6 or 7 year payment that you'll regret. By letting them do that, you're saying it's OK to take money from your pocket that could be used to pay bills or feed your family so they can feed theirs instead.

How the car dealer 'steals' your trade–in.

Car dealers live by two mottos: "All buyers are liars." and "Get full MSRP and 'steal' their trade."

The reason they say "All buyers are liars" is because dealers train their salespeople not to have any respect for the buyer's time or what they want to buy.

How they 'steal' your trade is by trying to wear you down mentally so that you to accept the value they come up with (see 'secret #1'). This is why they are happy when female or elderly buyers come alone without any support.

Those types of buyers almost always unsuspectingly get caught in a sandwich, with the salesperson and his manager on either side, pressuring them to accept a lower price than their trade–in is worth. The buyer eventually gives in from sheer exhaustion and feeling intimidated.

 **#20 "Market adjustment?" This is a joke, right?**

You visit a Chevy dealer and see that brand new hard to find Corvette. The greedy dealer has the nerve to ask as much as $20,000 over MSRP. This additional $20,000 is what's called 'market adjustment' or 'second sticker' pricing because there is a second sticker on the car showing MSRP and the extra $20,000.

C'mon, this is a Chevy not a Ferrari. Only complete idiots with money to throw away, or real old guys who have never heard of the internet, pay second sticker.

Go home turn on your computer and buy from one of the two largest Corvette dealers in America: Kerbeck and Macmulkin. Both are located on the East Coast and have more realistic pricing along with a large inventory to pick from. They will sell the Corvette to you for way less than second sticker and ship it to wherever you want.

A car loan is like a home loan with wheels.

#21

Buying a car and a home are similar in the sense that if you obtain financing for the purchase, that type of financing is a 'mortgage'.

For a car this is actually called a 'chattel mortgage' which is an old English law legal term for financing of moveable goods.

'Secret' $1,000 General Motors coupons.

General Motors issues incentive coupons to their dealers that have a cash value of $500 or $1,000.

Dealers have discretion to use them toward your down payment. They get these coupons every month and the quantity received depends on how many cars they sell. Dealers who sell more cars get more coupons.

When you get close to negotiating a new car deal and are only $1,000 or so away from it becoming a reality, ask the dealer if they have any incentive coupons that can be applied toward your purchase.

If a dealer has them they will claim only one can be used per buyer, however, that isn't exactly true. They can call their General Motors rep and get permission to use more if they're desperate enough to earn your business.

KBB, NADA or Mannheim. Which to use?

When trying to estimate the value of their trade–in, most people are familiar with Kelley Blue Book (KBB) or NADA. They assume that those values are the most accurate in determining car value.

Dealers generally depend on Mannheim Auto Auction appraisal figures more than KBB or NADA.

Why? Because Mannheim values accurately reflect *real time* auto auction amounts other dealers are willing to pay whereas KBB and NADA do not. This is why your neon Volkswagen Beetle with the eyelashes and flower vase will have a higher trade–in value using KBB or NADA when in fact it should be much less.

KBB and NADA don't buy or sell vehicles whereas the Mannheim auto auction figures give the most up-to-date price being paid for the vehicle.

The BEST time to buy a car.

There are many articles online advising the 'best' time to buy a car. Honestly speaking, the best time is when you are actually ready to make the purchase.

Why do I say this? I read an article once. It said the best time to buy a car is always on a rainy day at the end of the month. I think this is a great idea but likely to fail if the dealer has met his sales quota that day and isn't anxious to sell a car at a deep discount.

If no sales were made that day (this happens quite often) the sales manager will include his first born as part of the deal if it will result in being able to record a sale before close of business.

And the WORST time to buy a car.

Walking into the dealership with a smile on your face 20 minutes before they close knowing that you are holding everyone up.

After working a 12 hour grind, nobody likes some schmuck coming in at the last minute keeping them there even longer so that they can't get home to their family.

Jerks like that lose every single time even though they might not know it. Don't make the salesperson, their manager, and the guy getting paid minimum wage who must stay late to clean your new car, hate you more than they already do.

There are plenty of ways to skin a cat and you'll be skinned many times over pulling a stunt like that.

Ask to see the lending bank rate sheet.

Today all car dealers are networked online with banks, credit unions and hard money lenders on standby to approve loans. This helps them maintain control over you and the sales transaction.

Once you get approved, ask to see the 'rate sheet' for the lender they are using. Reviewing the rate sheet confirms the car dealer did not increase your interest rate to make an additional profit.

The interest rate quoted on the rate sheet should be the same as what appears in the financing documents. If it doesn't have them print new documents with the correct figures.

0% financing. All dealers have it.

First of all, banks do NOT offer 0% financing, why would a bank lend you money for 0% just to have you as a customer? This type of financing is always provided by the car manufacturer with 2 exceptions:

1. If you have bad credit, a dealer will charge you full MSRP so they could use part of their profit to 'buydown' the rate to 0%. Buydown is a fancy way of saying they will pre-pay part of the interest to make sale so you can get the 0%.

2. The same goes for people with great credit who expect to receive 0% financing when the manufacturer is not offering it that month. They will be expected to let the dealer make more of a profit so part of it can be used to buydown their interest rate.

Joke of the day: "I want your best price."

Why would you walk in and tell a dealer you want his 'best' price because you are going to take that offer and see if another dealer can do better?

People do this all the time and it just doesn't make sense. They assume the dealer is so anxious for their business that they will play this silly game.

Nobody is going to give you their best offer to shop around so you can return later and ask them to beat the best price they already gave you.

This type of question shows the dealer you are inexperienced at negotiating and don't know what you're talking about. Some might give you an offer but most will say "Thanks for coming in." and watch you leave.

Leasing: Demand a high residual value.

In your lease contract, residual value is the amount you can purchase your vehicle for if you want to buy it when the lease is over. Residual values are determined by the bank and vary depending on the vehicle.

The higher the residual value, the lower your monthly lease payment.

If the residual value is 57% of MSRP, your lease payments will be higher than if the residual value were 63% of MSRP. This is because at 57% you are paying for the remaining 43% of the vehicle original value.

If the residual value is 63%, you are paying for the remaining 37% of the vehicle original value.

Leasing lets you get more vehicle for less money plus you get to change cars every three years.

If you hold on to a car and drive it until the wheels fall off you're not a leasing candidate.

Smell coffee? It was a smoker's car.

Trade-in vehicles often have smells that over the years settle into the cloth or leather and can't be removed with simple air freshener.

Dealers try to cover up the odor inside of a bad smelling used car by wrapping fresh ground coffee in a tissue or paper towel and hiding it under the seat

During a test drive, you'll be distracted by the fresh coffee smell which quickly wears off soon after you buy the car. By then it's too late because the dealer has your money.

The only guaranteed way to get rid of bad odors in a used car is to use an ozone generator but most dealers refuse to buy one because it's expensive.

Buy from a "Mom and Pop" lot or a franchise?

Don't buy from small one location lots. Their cars are mostly rejects purchased from car auctions that a franchised (e.g. Ford, General Motors, Honda, Subaru, etc.) dealer would never consider for resale because of their poor condition.

These are called 'Pop lots' which is short for 'Mom and Pop'. Ignorant salespeople will often call them 'pot lots' because they don't know what they're talking about but try to sound like they do.

Buy from a 'Pop lot' and good luck getting help from them if that "As is" $3,500 car you bought for your 16 year old breaks down after you leave.

Why YOU should pick the test drive route.

Car salespeople are told by their manager to only use certain roads and highways for the test drive. If you notice, these routes are very flat and have seldom have bumps.

The intent of controlling your drive this way is to ensure that you don't go up a steep hill and realize the car doesn't have enough torque (i.e. enough acceleration to push you up the hill without straining the engine), or go over any bumps which might demonstrate how harsh the suspension is under those conditions.

There is another reason the salesperson is told to control where you drive.

If they think you're a 'brick' they will give you a longer 'good credit' drive but if they think you're a 'roach' you get to drive a mile or two and that's it because from your looks they assume you have bad credit and won't qualify for a car loan.

Test drive for at least 15 minutes.

Buyers make the costly mistake of letting the car salesperson give them a 5 or 10 minute test drive. This is because salespeople are pressured to have the buyer act impulsively and not think logically about the car buying transaction.

Your test drives MUST always be a minimum of 15 minutes for each and every vehicle that you are seriously considering buying, especially if switching from a sedan to a SUV.

A lengthy test drive gives extra time to have a real life driving experience and discover any problems that only arise after driving the car for a long period, i.e. uncomfortable seats or blind spots.

The government allows deceptive car ads.

We've all seen those new car ads offering as bait the very low monthly payment in BIG print and 'gotcha' conditions in SMALL print (large cash down payment, near perfect credit score, etc.) that most people miss.

This type of advertising is misleading and does nothing to enhance the car dealer's reputation in the eyes of the public. The auto industry lobby is so powerful that the Federal Trade Commission (FTC) and Consumer Financial Protection Bureau (CFPB) refuse to clean up this mess because our politicians are bought and sold by lobbyists who represent the manufacturers instead of the people who voted them into office.

When responding to these ads, pay extremely close attention to all the conditions so you aren't disappointed when it comes to actually making a purchase.

Keep your keys. Don't be held hostage.

#35

If you are trading in your car, the salesperson will ask for its keys so their used car manager can examine it.

While this is a perfectly legitimate request, letting them take possession of your keys allows them to hold you hostage while they try to pressure you into buying.

A better way is to accompany the manager to your car, and get in if he wants to drive it. When he finishes you immediately take back your keys so they are not 'lost' or 'misplaced' while you negotiate price.

ALWAYS
test drive the car
you plan to buy.

No two cars, even if they are the same brand with similar options, ride the same way even though a salesperson will say they do.

Make sure to test drive the actual car you intend to buy because there can be subtle but very important differences in the handling.

If you place a deposit on a car that you have not test driven, make sure the contract has a clause that your money will be refunded in full if for any reason at time of delivery you are not satisfied with how the car handles and the problem (that should be covered under warranty) cannot be corrected to *your satisfaction* by the dealer service department.

Did you feel that? You were just "4–payed"!

A "1-pay" is a $250 commission, $500 is called a "2-pay", etc. A '4-pay' ($1,000 commission) is the Holy Grail and happens when:

1. The buyer is a bad negotiator who pays more than necessary,

2. Accepts a low value for their trade-in (this is called 'under allowing the trade') and,

3. Has really bad credit and is desperate to get a car.

These three conditions together create a 'perfect storm' where the salesperson could make $1,000 or more from the transaction.

Be the big fish that got away, not the one that they land and eat for dinner.

Look stupid, then ask to see the invoice

Never, pay full MSRP for your car. Before signing any commitment to purchase, ask to see a copy of the dealer invoice.

Use it to check the difference between actual MSRP and the invoice price so you can learn how much profit the dealer hopes to make.

You should pay as close to the invoice price as possible, OR even below invoice if you are a strong negotiator and dealing with a salesperson whose manager is desperate to make a sale.

When to use the dealer service department.

If you use the dealer service department, there will be a written history of how well you took care of your car by bringing it in for the required oil changes and any other scheduled maintenance. It might be a bit more expensive but helps increase the value of your trade–in if you decide to buy another car from the same dealer.

The more history you develop by having the same dealership service your car, the better your chances of qualifying to receive future discounted service coupons in the mail or online.

A dealer is also more likely to give you better pricing on a new car because they hope they'll recover that discount through work performed by their service department.

Why a long term loan costs more.

In macroeconomics, the term 'rent' is used to call the interest people pay for borrowing money. For example, the interest (rent) for a 48 month loan will be less than for a 72 month loan.

The longer your loan term the higher your interest will be. That's because with a longer loan term, there is greater risk to the lender of some event (loss of job, death, divorce) happening to prevent the borrower from making timely repayment.

What is a "WE OWE"?

When buying a car there might be some accessory, like an extra key, trailer hitch or bike rack the dealer has promised to provide.

If the item cannot be included at the time of delivery, the dealer must issue to you what is called a "WE OWE' form. On the "WE OWE" they list the items they still owe you that have already been paid for separately or rolled into the financed amount.

Get a "WE OWE' before leaving. Don't rely on the dealer verbal assurances or you'll never get what was promised.

Check the dealer used car online price.

Ever visit a car dealership and see a sticker on the car giving one price, then you check online to see a much lower price, sometimes a few thousand dollars less, for the exact same stock number?

Management encourages salespeople to purposely quote you the higher sticker price hoping you don't look online before agreeing to buy the car. In some states there is no recourse if you unknowingly pay higher than the online ad price so B-E-W-A-R-E.

Used car inspection report – get a copy.

#43

Don't take the word of the salesperson. Ask to review a copy of the used car inspection report completed by the service department. By examining this, you know exactly what work was done before the car was offered for sale.

The report is usually signed by the service department manager. This document is very important, especially if you end up buying a car that is supposed to be a Certified Pre–Owned vehicle.

If mechanical problems develop after the purchase, the dealer's inspection report will document what parts of the car were examined and/or replaced.

Often a busy service department does a sloppy inspection, or none at all, then puts on the report that certain work was done when it wasn't. If they attest to something like this in their written report and information is false, you are a victim of fraud and have legal recourse.

Slow down ... read all of your documents.

Buying a new car costs thousands of dollars so take time to read every single document the finance manager is asking you to sign while in their office.

A common trick is to hurry the buyer through the signing process THEN put all their papers in an envelope and either tape or staple it shut.

The reason for this is most buyers don't bother to open the envelope after they get home to review what they signed. Sometimes it will sit in the glove compartment unopened for months.

This kind of delay may cause a buyer to lose the chance to cancel unwanted additional services they were pressured into buying because the deadline to cancel has expired.

New car customer survey. You're in charge.

When you buy a new car, the salesperson will tell you to expect a survey from the manufacturer and to please give the dealership maximum scores in every category.

The salesperson is under pressure to get a high score, a '10' in every category, even those they have no control over, otherwise the dealership withholds performance bonuses from their pay. It's another slimy dealer tactic that is grossly unfair to the salesperson but could work to your advantage.

If you receive a survey and for some reason aren't happy, contact the salesperson or their manager and express your concern. This can be a win–win situation for everyone. You get the 'problem' taken care of (e.g. the dealer bribes you with a full tank of gas) and the salesperson gets a high survey score so their pay is not cut.

The price that dealers hate to disclose.

In most states dealers are required by law to post the asking price of a used car on the car itself or they must pay a fine. The purpose of this law is so that a buyer knows upfront what the true asking cost is.

Many dealers refuse to do this and gamble that the state attorney general is too busy to catch them. Don't let the dealer use your lack of information to have you pay more. Ask why the price is not posted on the car.

The state Attorney General is your friend.

Every state Attorney General's office has a consumer protection division. They are mostly understaffed and can't be aware of every problem all the time.

If you have trouble with the car dealer that involves false advertising, bait and switch or issues related to your purchase contract for a new or used car, report the dealer immediately.

Don't waste valuable time and energy trying to negotiate with a dealer whom you believe is not acting in good faith.

While the dealer might delay responding to you, they don't want their license or franchise to be at risk with the Attorney General, neither do they want to attract the attention of the local TV reporter who wants to make a name for themselves from exposing the dealer's shady business practices.

Why salespeople hate telephone questions.

#48

Salespeople at every dealership are evasive when you call to ask simple questions about a specific vehicle … especially if it's about the *price*.

That's because they are told by their sales manager NOT to answer direct questions, just get an appointment for you to come in.

While this isn't necessarily a bad thing, more often than not they do NOT have the car you called about and will try to switch you to another vehicle when you visit. This is called a 'bait and switch' and it's illegal but happens all the time in the car business.

Before driving to the dealer, ask the salesperson text or email you a recent photo of the vehicle in question. This will at least give some assurance they still have it for sale – and make it harder for the dealer to claim it was sold a few minutes before you got there.

What is dealer 'pack' on cars?

The 'pack' is the upfront fixed amount of estimated overheard a dealership will deduct before they compute the salesperson's commission, usually on a used car.

For example, assume the pack is $500. If the salesman earns the dealership a $2,000 profit on the used car sale, his commission will be based on $1,500.

U R female?
Wham, Bam,
Thank you Ma'am!

Dealers become orgasmic when a woman visits their showroom alone to buy a car. Why? Because they know they can prey on her vulnerability. When a woman shops by herself, they know there is a better chance of pressuring her into buying what they want, ***instead of selling her what she wants***.

Women who shop alone for a car are more likely to be pressured into buying something they don't really want if the dealer is able to delay them long enough and wear them down.

Since few women are really adept at assessing the mechanical condition of the used car, they are more likely to buy one with defects the dealer chose not to fix before offering the car for sale. When buying a used car women (and men too) should have their own mechanic examine the car before committing to buy.

The "4–square". Don't sign it ... yet.

#51

The "4-square" is a sheet of paper the salesperson uses to negotiate pricing with you.

The 4-square is called that because it shows 4 pieces of information essential to the transaction that are laid out in 4 squares: **1)** car price, **2)** down payment, **3)** value of your trade–in (if applicable) and **4)** monthly payment and term.

Dealers stay up nights losing sleep trying to figure out 4-square scams to confuse you so they can maximize their profit.

Don't sign a 4-square, or even initial one, until all the terms you wanted are shown ***and the interest rate based on approved credit after your credit report is pulled is shown too***. Even though the salesperson will claim it's not legally binding, signing a 4-square means you are 'in principle' committing to terms as presented.

How to cancel a factory order.

Let's say a dealer talks you into placing a factory order then collects a "non-refundable" deposit from you. The car takes 8 – 12 weeks for delivery.

In the meantime you find a different vehicle elsewhere and want to cancel your factory order and get your money back. The dealer says your deposit is forfeited.

If a VIN number has not been assigned to your factory order car, the dealer cannot legally keep your deposit because it's for a car that does not exist. Your deposit must be returned. If they refuse see a lawyer or call your state Attorney General consumer protection division.

Dealer magic can INCREASE the interest rate.

Your actual credit score might qualify you for 0.9% financing instead of 1.9%.

Not being savvy to how car loan financing works, you go into the finance office and sign papers for a loan at 1.9% interest when actually it should be 0.9%. You were just scammed into paying an extra 1% ... more profit to the dealer!

The finance manager won't volunteer that you can receive a lower interest rate. Why? Because they work for the dealer and get a bonus for getting you to accept paying the higher interest rate.

Review the lending bank rate sheet ('secret' #26) applicable to your credit score then confront the dealer if they are charging an interest rate that is more than what you came up with.

A clean trade–in NEVER increases its value.

All the time I see people spending a couple of hundred dollars to have their trade–in detailed assuming it will receive a higher appraisal from the dealer when they buy a new car.

The dealer isn't interested in how clean and shiny your car is. Their only concerns are the condition of the engine and how much damage there is to the inside and outside that needs repair.

Keep that cash in your pocket.

Intimidation tactic: the 'silent appraisal'.

This is a psychological trick designed to intimidate people trading in their car.

When examining the trade–in for damages etc., the salesperson is told to have the buyer standby and watch while they run their hand over any damage to the car.

The salesperson is told to occasionally grunt or frown with disapproval at every scratch, ding or dent they write down on their notepad. The idea is to make buyer uncomfortable and believe their trade–in won't be worth as much as they were hoping and accept whatever is offered.

Using the 'Columbo'. Are they serious? LOL!

Old time car dealers want their salespeople to do the 'Columbo' when negotiating price. This silly technique is based on the NBC TV series from the 70's with Peter Falk who starred as a police detective, Lt. Columbo, who wore a ratty raincoat.

Columbo would turn to walk away from a suspect, take two steps then turn around and make a comment to unnerve the suspect so they would know he figured out how they committed the crime.

When a salesperson does the 'Columbo', they take the buyer's offer and turn away.

After taking two steps, the salesperson is supposed to turn around like Columbo and say "I'm not sure if this offer will work but I'll do my best."

The idea is to somehow create concern in the buyer that their offer might be rejected and prepare them to offer more money. Really???

Don't combine new car and trade-in pricing.

Discuss each issue separately. First finalize the purchase price of the new car THEN discuss how much you will accept for your trade.

Every car dealer will try to negotiate both transactions together, don't let them.

Why do they insist on doing this? Because if they give you a discount on the car you want to buy, they will try to offer less for your trade to recover the discount they just agreed to.

This is an old trick to throw you off guard so pay attention.

If they refuse to negotiate each transaction separately just go to another dealer.

Listen to the radio then turn it OFF.

Car salespeople try to hide the road noise in a new or used car by turning up the radio during your test drive.

Before you leave the lot, check out the audio system to make sure that it works. After that, turn it off for the rest of the demo. You want to hear the engine and be on the lookout for any unusual noises that might scream "Don't buy me!"

"I'm working on your behalf." Yeah, right.

If a car salesperson says they're working for you, don't walk, run out the door. It's a gross misrepresentation and an insult to your intelligence.

The salesperson is an employee of the dealer, not the buyer. This means they are the dealer's agent and not yours.

By law the salesperson can only work on behalf of the person who gives them their paycheck.

They can't work on your behalf and the dealer's at the same time. Don't fall for this phony attempt to win you over.

You want a discount for paying cash? LMAO!

#60

Don't expect a discount for paying cash to buy a car because won't get a discount – ever.

Think about it. **Why** would a car dealer give you a discount for paying cash? Do you ask that when buying groceries at Safeway? No.

This is a stupid question that tells a car dealer the one thing which will piss them off: they won't be able to make extra money off you with a financing kickback from the lender plus the financing manager won't be able to sell you an overpriced warranty package. Now you want a discount? The dealer will work even harder to find some other way to get more money out of you.

How do you handle this? Tell them you are financing the car. After all the terms of the purchase are finalized then say you're paying cash.

The first one to give a number loses.

When negotiating your purchase, sit back and let the salesperson do all the talking so you can observe how anxious they are to make the sale.

Make sure they put their complete offer in writing for you to review. Do not rely on verbal assurances because the dealer will always deny having offered those terms and then try to change the terms to make more money off you.

If you do all the talking first, they'll know exactly how much you can afford to pay and will never offer their best pricing.

Yes, we (really don't) have that car.

Ever call a dealership about a specific car they have advertised only to be told when you arrive that it's in service, being test driven, etc. and they try to switch you to a different vehicle?

That car was already sold when you called or never existed in the first place. These are usually one-of-a-kind "bait cars", also referred to in the industry more politely as "ad cars". Only one ad car is ever available to purchase. If more than one is offered then the trim level and options are different. A dealer knows from experience that most buyers will not see the fine print disclosing that only one car is offered at that price. This is another slimy and unethical trick to have you rush in with hopes you can be talked into picking a different vehicle.

An ad car will always be offered at a ridiculously low price. The dealer will do their best NOT to sell it if it's still there when you show up to buy it. They need this car to bring in buyers like yourself so they can try and switch them to a different higher priced vehicle. Don't be surprised if the ad car was sold by the time you arrive to buy it, it usually is.

This tactic is called a 'bait and switch' which is illegal and should be immediately reported to your state Attorney General.

"Yes, I plan to use your service department."

Dealers make most of their income from activity generated by their service department, not selling new cars.

When negotiating buying a new car, always tell the dealer you plan to use their service department for any work that needs to be done.

They will agree to give you a further price reduction if they think they can make even more money off you from oil changes and other maintenance after the car is sold.

Get a second opinion on all repair quotes.

If you need major repair work done on your car, always get a second opinion to ensure the dealer is not over charging you for the work to be done.

Dealers are notorious for saying they do in-house repair work when actually they are sending the car to an independent garage that will do the work and give them a kickback.

The dealer then tacks on their profit to whatever the repair shop quoted and you end up paying more than you should.

Dealer verbal abuse means desperation.

You can gauge how desperate the dealer is to make a sale by how they treat you.

A conversation can quickly turn from friendly banter to them insulting your credit score (if you have bad credit), or saying you can easily afford to buy the car (if you have good credit) and ask why you are haggling over several hundred dollars.

That money is just as good in your bank account as it is theirs. If after making a reasonable offer you are verbally abused, just get up and walk out.

More often than not they will call you before the day is over, especially if sales are slow, and accept your terms.

Maintain control and let them chase you, not the other way around.

Use your own insurance agent, not theirs!

If the buyer doesn't have insurance coverage, the salesperson will eagerly offer to 'help' by conveniently referring them to an insurance agent.

What the salesperson doesn't tell you is that they get a referral kickback from the insurance agent, as much as $200.

To add insult to injury, the agent places your coverage with a company that costs way more than one you can easily find on your own.

The dealer is taking advantage of you as it is and don't fall for this scam. Find an insurance agent yourself.

'Bump' yourself and it will cost you plenty!

When a salesperson talks you into increasing the monthly payment you say you can afford to pay, this is called a 'bump'.

For example you say "I can only afford to pay $250 per month."

The salesperson responds by saying, "OK. You can afford to pay $250 per month *up to* what amount?"

If you respond by saying "Up to $275." this is called a 'bump' because you were tricked into increasing your monthly payment from $250 to $275.

Do the math. If you get a 60 month auto loan, you have allowed the dealer to make an extra $1,500 (60 x $25 = $1,500) because you were tricked into paying another $25 per month.

Get $10,000
for unauthorized
credit pull.

Check your state consumer laws regarding identity theft. If you visit a car dealer and they pull your credit report <u>before</u> you sign the credit application and privacy notice, you might be able to collect as much as $10,000 in damages for their carelessness.

The dealer can legally ask you to submit an online credit application but they should not be completing your credit application over the telephone since they don't know who they are speaking with.

Bad credit and loan shark lending rates.

People with bad credit pay a higher interest rates. This doesn't necessarily mean their interest rate must always be in the stratosphere but dealers want you to believe that.

Why? If they get you approved by a high rate lender, you won't complain because you already thought you couldn't get a car loan.

You might be paying an extra 5% on your interest rate for no legitimate reason other than the dealer is taking advantage of your fear.

Don't rush to sign unethical contracts which have a high interest rate and all kinds of penalties.

Take your time and see if you can get more reasonable financing without using the dealer's lender.

Use social media to keep the dealer honest.

Car dealers love social media as a means for happy customers to post a message about their positive experience. They hate social media if an unsatisfied buyer posts anything negative about how the dealer treated them.

One negative posting on Yelp will make most dealers sweat and do everything possible to please the customer so the negative review will either be deleted or upgraded to positive.

Consider using social media as a way to make the dealer treat you fairly and respectfully.

Avoiding an unwanted test drive.

The attitude of all dealerships is that if you set foot on their lot that means you want to buy their car N-O-W.

To them there is no such thing as comparison shopping or browsing. Dealers teach their salespeople that all buyers are liars and when you say "No, I'm not buying right now." that really means, "Yes, I want to buy your car before I leave."

Salespeople are watched through one-way glass and/or closed circuit TV by management. They are pressured to have you test drive the car then come inside to negotiate pricing even if you don't want to.

If you tell the salesperson you are just shopping and not ready to buy, they will not listen and still focus on getting a test drive.

One way is to ask you sit next to them in the car while they offer to show you some 'special' feature of the car.

Once you're inside they will drive off to a nearby parking lot then have you sit in the driver's seat to force a test drive.

It sounds crazy but this is a tactic many dealerships tell their people to use with hopes that you'll change your mind and decide to buy after driving the car back to the dealership.

Setting you up for the finance manager.

Some dealerships pressure their salespeople to try and convince you to buy a warranty or service contract from the finance manager when you sign your loan documents.

These packages are expensive and really designed for the finance manager to make a commission off you. They will even go so far as to say they are required by the manufacturer.

Don't be deceived by the friendliness of the salesperson if they suggest buying any of these programs. They've taken enough of your money.

Limited English?
Bring a translator.

Car dealers love non-English speaking buyers. If they have a salesperson on staff who can understand the language, the salesperson wins the buyer's trust and uses it to overcharge them for their car and offer them less for their trade–in.

That same salesperson will also sit with the buyer when they go into the finance manager to convince them all the documents are "OK", endorse purchasing the overpriced extended warranty coverage and sign all the paper work without asking any questions. In some states this is called a conflict of interest.

Deals like this usually generate a '4-pay' ($1,000 commission or more) for the salesperson and thousands in profit for the dealership.

If the buyer can't speak English, they should bring someone familiar with car buying who can negotiate on their behalf,

The Statue of Limitations and old debt.

#74

The statute of limitations for a debt is the period of time that a creditor or collector can ask the court to force you to pay it. The time period starts on that account's date of last activity. Each state has its own statute of limitations on debt.

The statute of limitations varies depending on the type of debt you have and is usually between three and six years, but can be up to 10 years or more.

Before you respond to a debt collector or anyone else contacting you about an old debt, find out what the statute of limitations is in your state.

If you fail to do this first, you might restart the statute of limitations by mistake which would legally extend the amount of time the debt collector can take action in court against you.

Get a FREE copy of your credit report.

Don't waste money paying services for a copy of your credit report. The Federal Trade Commission says you're entitled to receive ONE free copy of your credit report every 12 months from each of the three nationwide credit reporting companies: Equifax, Experian and TransUnion. You can order your reports online from:

www.annualcreditreport.com

It is the only authorized website for free credit reports, or call **1-877-322-8228**.

You must provide your name, address, social security number, and date of birth to verify your identity. If ordering online, be sure to download or print a copy of each report since there is no way to save it after you access the file.

How to kill 'zombie' debt collectors.

Zombie debt collectors are large corporations who buy charged off debt from the original owner. They buy this old unpaid debt for between 1 and 3 cents on the dollar then try to collect the full amount from you.

Often the debt is so old that the statute of limitations has expired but the debt collector won't tell you this. They will try to win your cooperation by asking for a token payment which would restart the already expired statute of limitations.

If a zombie debt collector contacts you to collect a debt that is time barred (i.e. they can no longer sue you in court) by the statute of limitations, drive a stake through their heart by reporting them immediately to the Consumer Financial Protection Bureau **www.cfpb.gov** who will investigate the matter further.

'Re-aging' credit report debt is illegal.

Another trick that debt collectors use is change the date of last activity of an old account on your credit report to make it appear more recent.

Your account date of last activity might be in 2004 and no longer collectible under the statute of limitations but the collector changes the date to 2015 which is when they bought the debt.

They do this so they have more time to take aggressive collection efforts against you and gamble you don't check your credit reports regularly enough to see what they did.

Changing the date of last activity on an old account to make it appear new is called "re-aging" and is prohibited by federal law. If you catch a company doing this you have legal recourse because they deliberately filed fraudulent information on your credit report. Make sure to print a copy of the credit report and consult with a lawyer.

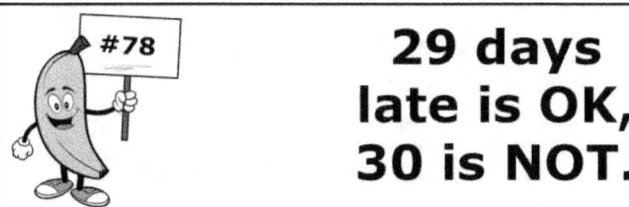

Most people panic and believe their loan, credit card or mortgage account will be shown as delinquent on the credit report if their payment arrives even one day past the due date.

Relax. Credit bureaus don't show your payments as late until they are **30 days past the agreed payment date**; for student loans, Navient will only show them as late if you are 90 days late or more.

Remember this if cash is tight and you need a few extra days to get the payment in. While this strategy will help you squeeze some extra time to pay the bill, it won't prevent you from accruing late fees and extra interest charges for missing the payment date.

How to pay 0% interest on credit card debt.

If you have a credit score of 720 or higher, apply to banks that are offering 0% interest ***if you open a credit card with them and transfer your unpaid credit card balances***.

Some banks offer grace periods as long as 21 months at 0% if you agree to become their customer.

Before the grace period is almost over, apply at another bank who offers 0% for transferring your balances to ***their*** credit card.

Using this strategy you might be able to go as long as 3 years or more without paying any interest while reducing your balances. Use the money you save by not paying interest to pay more on your credit card balance(s) at the bank's expense!

Never file a credit report dispute online.

If you review your credit reports online, always make a copy for your records. These records will also be helpful in case you disagree with the accuracy of any items that are shown.

The 3 major credit reporting agencies (Equifax, Experian, and TransUnion) offer a procedure to file an online dispute but don't use it. Use 'secret' #87 for details on how to submit a dispute to the credit bureau like the professionals do.

How to delete an IRS lien off a credit report.

Is that federal tax lien on your credit report killing your FICO score and preventing you from getting a new credit card or loan? Getting the IRS to remove it is easy.

If as an individual taxpayer you owe $50,000 or less, and agree to let the IRS deduct that tax over a term of up to 72 months directly from your bank account, you should be able to get the tax lien deleted from your credit report without using a lawyer or credit repair company. Here is the process:

Complete and submit to the IRS Form 433-D "Installment Agreement". It takes about 45 days before the first installment is be deducted from your account.

After 3 consecutive monthly installments have been deducted, it's time to file IRS Form 1227 "Application for Withdrawal of Filed Form 668(Y), Notice of Federal Tax Lien.

Within 30 days of receiving Form 12277, the IRS will instruct the credit bureaus to remove the tax lien from your credit report!

The lien will not reappear as long as the IRS is able to successfully deduct installments from your bank account.

If you default on your agreement, the IRS will refile the tax lien and it will reappear on your credit report.

While the process is slow (about 4 months), it's legitimate and will work 100% of the time. Use these links to download the necessary IRS Forms:

Form 433-D:

http://www.irs.gov/pub/irs-pdf/f433d.pdf

Form 12277:

http://www.irs.gov/pub/irs-pdf/f12277.pdf

"You're pre-approved"? Sort of.

We've all received "pre-approved" credit offers in the mail.

How do we get selected? Banks and loan companies don't actually pull your credit report, they pay the credit bureau to give them the names and addresses of people whose credit score fits their criteria.

Some offers are for credit with very low interest rates while others read like they're coming from a loan shark. You're "pre-approved" with final approval subject to the bank or loan company actually pulling your credit report to review the content.

For each pre-approval solicitation you respond to you lose about 5 points off your credit score.

What's even worse is that by the bank pulling your credit, an inquiry stays on your file for 2 years.

Be selective about which pre-approval solicitations you answer. Too many inquiries on your credit report will cause you to lose points and also be denied by other lenders if they see you are applying for too much credit.

Keep the inquiries to no more than 3 within a 12 month period to avoid damaging your credit score or having your loan application turned down.

Experian credit bureau is foreign owned?!

Of the three major credit reporting agencies, Equifax and TransUnion are U. S. based.

The third company Experian is headquartered in Ireland… but has a U. S. subsidiary. Few U. S. citizens know that their personal credit information is controlled by Experian whose subsidiary once sold the credit information of hundreds of thousands of Americans to a foreign national that resold the data online.

Read about it in this article:

http://krebsonsecurity.com/2014/03/experian-lapse-allowed-id-theft-service-to-access-200-million-consumer-records/

#84
40 'reporting' agencies you never heard of.

Just about everyone has heard of Equifax, Experian and TransUnion but did you also know that there are more than 40 other consumer reporting agencies that collect and sell your personal information?

Download this free pamphlet to find out exactly who is watching you and what information they are selling to their subscribers:

http://files.consumerfinance.gov/f/201501_cfpb_list-consumer-reporting-agencies.pdf

Write, don't phone the credit bureau.

Send your letter via "Certified Mail, Return Receipt Requested". The clerk at the post office will show you which forms to use.

The cost will be about $7.00 but well worth it if the credit bureau doesn't respond and you need to file a formal complaint with the government about their failure to comply with the Fair Credit Reporting Act.

While you can sometimes call the credit bureau to discuss a problem, or use their online credit report dispute system, it won't receive the same kind of attention that a well written letter delivered by your friendly U. S. Postal Service does.

Never co-sign a loan for ANYONE!

#86

By co-signing for someone you are putting your own credit at risk in a number of ways:

If the person you co-signed for makes late payments, those late payments might show up on your credit history too since you are on record as the co-signer.

Co-signing for someone else's debt makes it harder for you to qualify for a credit card or other financing when you need it because your debt-to-income ratio might be too high.

If you any reason the person you co-signed for defaults on their payments, the creditor will immediately look to you for payment.

When you co-sign you are on the hook for the full loan term (with a car loan this could be 5 or 6 years) UNLESS you are confident the person you co-signed for will be able to qualify for financing on their own in the near future.

Instead of co-signing, consider placing the person on your credit card account(s) as an "Authorized User" but don't let them have the credit card, have it sent to you.

As an Authorized User, your positive payment history will appear on that person's credit report and hopefully increase their credit score enough for them to qualify on their own. This is a much safer way to help them than being their co-signer.

If the person who needs you to co-sign doesn't like to pay their bills, adding them to your accounts as Authorized User is most likely a waste of because their credit score will be so low this strategy to help improve it will not work.

Contact the credit card company and tell them who you want to add as an Authorized User (be sure to have their social security number) and your account should show on their credit report in about 10 days.

Delete
incorrect info
on your credit report.

Most people, including lawyers, mistakenly believe the Fair Credit Reporting Act (FCRA) says that negative information MUST stay on your credit report for 7 years.

This is NOT true. The FCRA says that by law most, but not all, derogatory information must be deleted from your credit report after 7 years, ***not that it must be reported for 7 years***.

If you feel there is an incorrect entry OR an old derogatory account is shown on your credit report, just send a letter to the credit reporting agency (by Certified Mail, Return Receipt Requested).

Tell them which account you believe has the wrong information or is outdated; they have 30 days to investigate and correct or delete the account and automatically send you a copy of the updated credit report as proof their action was completed.

Stopping debt collector harassment.

Lowlife debt collectors hire aggressive people who are paid minimum wage and a small commission on every dollar they collect from harassing you.

They call early morning or late at night, even on the weekends. You have probably received calls at work from a bill collector that has no regard for your privacy. At this link:

http://www.consumerfinance.gov/blog/debtcollectio n/

The Consumer Financial Protection Bureau has several letters you can use, depending on the situation, for dealing with an overly aggressive collection agency.

Avoid payday loan and check cashing scams.

Payday loan and check cashing services feed upon people with no bank account, or who have bad credit and are unable to open one or qualify for a loan.

Banks refuse to deal with this demographic so predatory lenders target that group by offering them their financial 'services'.

While there is definitely a need for this kind of resource, their annualized interest rates can be as high as 1,300% if someone uses them regularly.

Payday loans create a vicious cycle that prevent people from escaping because they must always renew their loan and use a portion of it again to pay an exorbitant fee for borrowing more money.

Forget the big banks. Join a credit union.

Unless you're Bill Gates or Warren Buffett, large banks (Chase, Bank of America, and Wells Fargo) don't care about you as a long term customer.

To them you are only as good as your last low interest yielding deposit that they use to loan to others at a much higher interest rate than they are paying you.

Credit unions are member owned and much easier to deal with. Plus they are not as rigid as a bank when considering your loan request.

Join a credit union instead of dealing with a major bank and reap the rewards of dealing with an organization that appreciates your business.

'Validate' the debt first.

If a collection agency contacts you, never agree to pay on any debt until they send proof the debt is yours.

A written request for this information is called a "validation letter" and must be sent to them Certified Mail, Return Receipt Requested within 30 days of being contacted.

In the validation letter ask for a copy of the original contract you signed as well as a full itemization of the amount they claim that you owe.

Also ask for proof from the owner of the debt that they are authorized to collect on their behalf.

Most collection agencies aren't able to provide this documentation because they don't have it, or because they know the Statute of Limitations has expired and they can't sue you.

Find out
who uses which
credit report.

Before applying for new credit, get copies of your credit reports to learn exactly what your scores are.

With this information in hand, call the car dealer, department store or place where you want credit and ask what credit bureau report they use.

This way you'll know in advance if they use the credit report that has your highest score.

Be careful not to have more than 3 or 4 inquiries showing per year on any report. This not only helps keep your score high but shows a potential creditor that you are not applying for credit at too many places.

Bankruptcy
is a
financial strategy.

Bad things can and do happen to good people, this includes filing for bankruptcy. Ignore the stigma that it used to have in the past, misfortune can occur which is beyond our control.

If you ever end up filing for bankruptcy, you must learn to think of it as a financial strategy and nothing more.

Fortune 1,000 corporations and even people like Donald Trump have filed for bankruptcy multiple times to reorganize their cash flow.

Do what you gotta to do. Nobody looks out for you better than you.

Partial payments might reactivate old debt.

Collection agencies are known for trying to scare people into paying old debt that their state Statute of Limitations says can no longer be collected.

Agreeing to a payment plan when you don't have to might possibly reactivate an old account so that it can re–appear as a new one on your credit report.

Consult with a lawyer before you make any commitment to pay debt that has expired because your state Statute of Limitations says the court can't make you pay it.

Warning:
Debt collectors
record your call.

Collection agencies record all conversations and in court they will try to use that information as evidence of a commitment from you to make payments.

Don't be tricked into having a phone conversation with these jerks. Tell them to communicate with you in writing.

FICO, Beacon or Empirica. Which is what?

When talking with a buyer who has just filled out a credit application, the car dealer might refer to the buyer's "Beacon" credit score as a standard for determining credit worthiness.

They fail to explain to the buyer what the "Beacon" is and which credit bureau it refers to.

In the U. S. there are 3 different credit rating agency scores that lenders use. They are:

FICO Score: Used by **Experian**, ranges between 330 and 830

Beacon Score: Used by **Equifax**, ranges between 300 and 850

Empirica Score: Used by **TransUnion**, ranges between 150 and 934

If a car dealer uses car dealer talk and says your "Beacon is 788", that is their way of saying they used your Equifax credit report to qualify you for a loan. Car dealers will usually use the Beacon (Equifax) or FICO (Experian) to determine how good someone's credit is.

Credit scores typically vary among credit bureaus because not all lenders want to incur the expense of reporting your payment history to all 3 credit bureaus.

How often should you check your credit reports?

#97

With identity theft being so rampant, you should check your TransUnion, Equifax and Experian credit scores at least once every 6 months to ensure all the accounts and balances belong to you and not someone else.

You don't lose points on your credit score for checking your own credit report.

Secured loans and cards boost credit scores.

One way of re-establishing bad credit is to apply for a secured loan. This used to be called a "passbook loan" during a time when people would hand over their passbook to the bank teller who would manually record their deposits and withdrawals.

With a secured loan you are borrowing money you already have on deposit which means there is no risk to the bank and your interest rate is lower.

This type of loan only takes a few minutes to process and banks usually lend up to 90% of your balance.

For example, if you have $500 on deposit, the bank will set aside the $500 in your account and loan you $450. Ask your bank which credit bureaus they report your loan to. If they refuse to give you a secured loan, then close your account and take your business elsewhere.

Make timely monthly repayments and the bank will report to the credit bureau your timely payment and your credit score will gradually improve.

You can also apply for a secured credit card and use it the same way as a secured loan. As long as you don't use more than 30% of your available credit, your credit score will jump over the next 6 months.

The 'Rule of 78' and interest payments.

Predatory lenders target uneducated and desperate borrowers with a method of calculating prepayment penalties on pre-computed auto loans (and other types of loans) called the Rule of 78s.

It's also referred to as the sum-of-the-digits because the sum of the digits 1 through 12 (1+2+3+4+5+6+7+8+9 +10+11+12) equal 78.

The Rule of 78s was created as a quick way for lenders to calculate extra charges for borrowers who paid their loans off early.

Today this method, sometimes called a 'pre-payment penalty' because the borrower is being penalized for paying off their loan early, is banned in some states but not all.

In states that don't have consumer friendly laws, it can still be found in installment loan and auto loan contracts.

When obtaining a car loan, particularly from "Buy Here Pay Here" lots, borrowers must ask to make sure it is not a Rule of 78s pre–computed auto loan.

If it is don't accept the financing and shop for a lending source that is more ethical and wants to earn your business.

Debit or credit. Which card is safer to use.

Contrary to popular belief, debit and credit cards are treated differently under consumer protection laws.

Per federal law, your personal liability for fraudulent charges on your CREDIT card cannot exceed **$50** but your personal liability for fraudulent charges on your DEBIT card could be **$500** or more, depending on how quickly you report it.

If you have bad credit, get a prepaid debit card at Walmart which is not tied to your regular checking or savings account.

Load money on to the Walmart card and use it for all of your purchases.

The goal is to safeguard your personal financial info as much as possible. Never use your regular debit card in restaurants, for car/hotel reservations or online purchases.

It is better for you if a hacker obtains your Walmart prepaid debit card info with little or no money on the card instead of your regular debit card which is tied to your checking account.

What is a 'hard' or 'soft' credit inquiry?

Hard inquiries occur when a car dealer, lender or credit card issuer, checks your credit report to make a lending decision. You must give the car dealer, lender or credit card issuer written permission to obtain a hard inquiry. Also note that hard inquiries lower your credit score by a few points and they may remain on your credit report for two years.

Soft inquiries are different and are generated when a person or company checks your credit report as part of a background check. Other examples include, getting "pre-approved" for credit card offers (a/k/a being on the 'sucker list') and checking your own credit score.

A soft inquiry can occur without your permission or knowledge unless you check your credit report. Soft inquiries won't affect your credit score.

Visit my website
askjoebananas.com

NOTES:

NOTES:

NOTES:

NOTES:

NOTES:

NOTES:

www.ingramcontent.com/pod-product-compliance
Lightning Source LLC
Chambersburg PA
CBHW060411290526
45791CB00002B/704